THE CHICAGO PUBLIC LIBRARY

DATE DUE

THE CHICAGO PUBLIC LIBRARY

ORIOLE PARK BRANCH
7454 W. BALMORAL
CHICAGO, IL 60656

Science Experiments

MOTION

by
John Farndon

BENCHMARK BOOKS

MARSHALL CAVENDISH
NEW YORK

Marshall Cavendish Corporation
99 White Plains Road
Tarrytown, New York 10591
© Marshall Cavendish Corporation, 2003

Created by Brown Partworks Limited

All rights reserved. No part of this book may be reproduced
or utilized in any form or by any means, electronic or mechanical,
including photocopying, recording, or by any information storage
and retrieval system, without prior written permission from the
copyright holders.

Library of Congress Cataloging-in-Publication Data

Farndon, John

Motion / by John Farndon
v. cm. — (Science experiments)
Includes index.
Contents: What is motion? — How fast? — Measuring speed — Getting faster —Understanding acceleration — Starting to move — Beating inertia — Force and acceleration — Friction — Rough and smooth — Action and reaction — Reaction rockets — High speed motion.
ISBN 0-7614-1471-1
1. Motion—Juvenile literature. 2. Motion—Experiments—Juvenile literature. [1. Motion—Experiments. 2. Experiments.] I. Title. II. Series.

QC133.5 .F37 2003
531'.11'078—dc21

2002005010

Printed in Hong Kong

PHOTOGRAPHIC CREDITS

CERN: p28
Corbis: p1, Raoul Minsart; p4, Raoul Minsart; p5, Bettman Archive; p23, Joel W Rogers
Daimler Christler: p6
Defense Link: p10/11
Empics: p14, Brian Drake; p20, Michael Steele; p22, Jon Buckle; p34, Chris Cole
Image Bank: p11, Yellow Dog Productions
NASA: p26
Pictor International: p16, p18
SSPL: p15, Science Museum
United States Professional Tennis Association, Inc: p9

Step-by-step photography throughout: Martin Norris

Front cover: Martin Norris

R03000187 97
Oriole Park Branch
7454 W. Balmoral Ave.
Chicago
DISCARD
Oriole Park Branch
7454 W. Balmoral Ave.
Chicago, IL 60656

Contents

WHAT IS MOTION?

Like every movement in the universe, a dramatic jump and kick obeys the same basic laws of motion worked out by scientists over the centuries.

Did you know?

Molecules are far too tiny to see, but they are always moving or at least vibrating, even when everything else is still. But if it gets very, very cold—down to minus 459.67°F (-273.15°C)—even molecules will stop moving. This theoretical temperature is called Absolute Zero.

In focus

ANCIENT GREEK IDEAS

Movement was first studied scientifically by the Ancient Greeks, over 2,000 years ago. It was the Greek thinker Aristotle (384-322 B.C.)—once tutor to Alexander the Great—who discovered the key role of force. Aristotle realized that things only start to move when pushed or pulled by a force. What Aristotle could not see was how things like arrows keep moving without force. Aristotle could see that it takes the force of an ox to pull a plow and the force of a bow to fire an arrow. Yet the ox must keep pulling to keep the plow moving—the arrow flies on by itself. Aristotle's ideas were built on by other Greek thinkers such as Archimedes, but it was 1,700 years before English scientist Isaac Newton found the answer.

Great Greek scientist Archimedes (287-212 B.C.) laid the foundations of the science of movement.

Everything in the universe is moving. Some movement is really obvious, like a car speeding along a highway, or a ball bouncing on the pavement. Other movement is less noticeable, like the whirling of the earth beneath our feet or the vibration of tiny atoms.

Without movement nothing would ever happen. Over the centuries scientists have given a great deal of attention and effort to how and why things move. In fact, there is a whole branch of science devoted to the study of movement, called dynamics. Scientists have discovered that nearly all movement obeys the same basic laws. Only things smaller than atoms behave differently.

Scientists who study movement use the word "motion" because it has a particular meaning. Motion is the change in position and orientation of an object.

When an object changes position, it moves from one place to another. Scientists call this motion translational. The simplest movement of this kind is linear motion, which means the object moves in a straight line. Linear motion can describe anything from a train on a railroad track to a raindrop falling from the sky.

When an object changes orientation it swivels to face in a different direction. Scientists describe this kind of motion as rotational, or simply as rotation.

HOW FAST?

Some things move so slowly it looks to human eyes as if they are still. The world's continents, for example, drift very slowly around the earth's surface, like ice on a pond. Yet since they move just an inch or so a year, it is only possible to detect the movement with sensitive laser satellite trackers.

On the other hand, many other things move so fast it is equally hard to see them moving. Even at relatively low speeds, some fast moving objects can become a blur, like the spinning wheels on a bicycle or vibrating guitar strings.The fastest thing in the universe is light, which can

150 years ago, the fastest people traveled on land was about 25 mph (40 km/h) on horse. Now speeds ten times this fast are common.

travel 186,000 miles (300,000 km) in just a second, and reach us from the Sun in less than eight minutes.

There are two measures of how fast something is traveling: speed and velocity. With speed, the direction of movement is not important. A bicycle's speed is simply how fast it is moving; it does not matter which way it is moving. Scientists call a simple rate like this a scalar quantity. Velocity shows how fast something is traveling in a particular direction. This is said to be a vector quantity.

Both velocity and speed are usually measured in terms of how far something travels in a regular time period—how many miles in an hour (mph or miles per hour), how many feet in a second (f/s or feet per second), and so on. Mathematically, velocity is the distance traveled divided by the time.

In practice, velocity can be measured only over a certain time and distance, however short. The time and distance are called limits. Theoretically, however, limits can be reduced to zero. Scientists then talk of instantaneous velocity. This is how fast something is moving at one instant—the instant a runner breaks the tape, say. In this instant, of course, no time passes so no distance is traveled, however fast the movement.

In the real world

SPEED COMPARISONS

Fingernails grow	0.02 in (0.05 cm) per week
Bacteria slither	0.00001 mph (0.00016 km/h)
Snails slide	0.005 mph (0.008 km/h)
Tortoises crawl	0.17 mph (0.27 km/h)
Fastest human sprints	34.3 mph (54.9 km/h)
Cheetah runs	63 mph (100 km/h)
Peregrine falcon dives	217 mph (350 km/h)
Fastest road car	217 mph (350 km/h)
Fastest helicopter	249 mph (400 km/h)
Tornado whirls	281 mph (450 km/h)
Fastest boat	319.6 mph (514.4 km/h)
Fastest train	320 mph (515 km/h)
Fastest jet car on land	633.5 mph (1,019 km/h)
Sound travels	760 mph (1,220 km/h)
Land speed record	763 mph (1,228 km/h)
Fastest airliner	1,600 mph (2,587 km/h)
Fastest jet plane	4,520 mph (7,274 km/h)
Space shuttle	16,600 mph (26,715 km/h)
Fastest humans have traveled, aboard *Apollo 10*	24,791 mph (39,897 km/h)
Earth orbits the Sun	66,620 mph (107,210 km/h)

Did you know?

Light is the fastest thing in the universe, traveling 299,792,458 meters per second (about 186,000 miles per hour). In fact, because scientists can measure the speed of light more accurately than they can a meter, they define a meter as 1/299,792,458 of the distance light travels in a second. Remarkably, unlike anything else, light's speed is always the same, no matter how or where you measure it, so scientists refer to the speed of light as a constant. Recently, though, researchers in Australia suggested that light may be getting slightly slower as the universe gets older.

MEASURING SPEED

You will need

- ✔ A stopwatch
- ✔ A small ball of modeling clay
- ✔ A couple of small pencils (to use as markers)
- ✔ A ball
- ✔ A tape measure

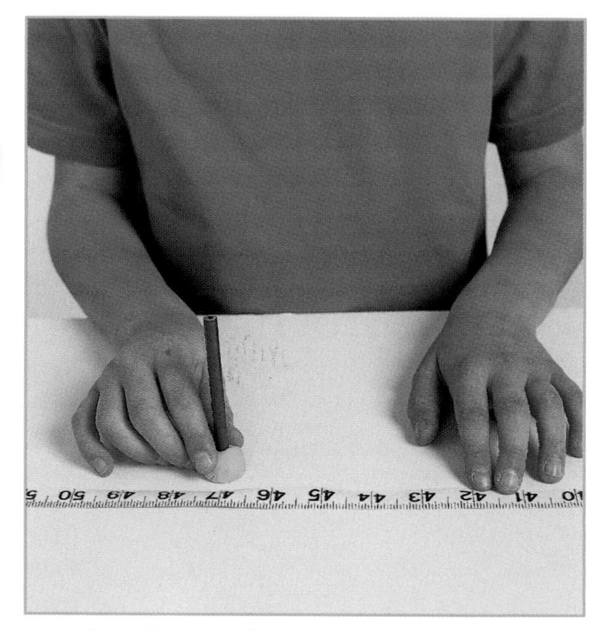

1 Stand a pencil in a blob of modeling clay to act as a marker. Measure out 10 ft (3 m) and set up another pencil.

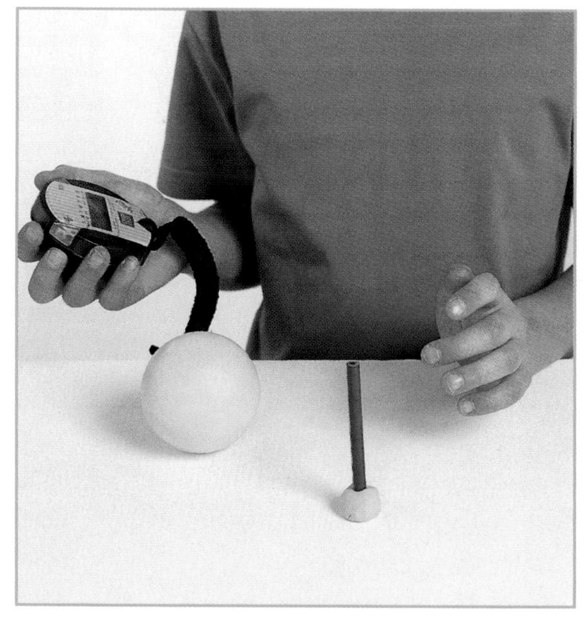

2 Roll the ball smoothly but quickly with one hand. Start the stopwatch just as it passes the marker pencil.

What is happening?

The speed or velocity of a moving object can be worked out from the time it takes to travel a particular distance. In this experiment, the distance the ball travels is 10 ft (3m). If the ball takes 2 seconds to complete the course, its speed is 10 ft in 2 seconds. To make speed comparisons, however, you need to know how far the ball travels in a standard time, such as 1 second. To work this out, simply divide the distance by the number of seconds, here 2. 10 divided by 2 is 5, so the speed is 5 feet per second. In this way, you can easily compare the speed of the ball over different runs and different distances.

In the real world

SPEED GUNS

Speed guns were originally developed for the police to see if cars were speeding. Now they have been adapted to measure speeds in sport—from a baseball pitch to a tennis serve. They work by emitting radar waves and detecting them as they bounce back from the ball. The gun works out the speed from how much the returning waves are stretched or squeezed by the movement of the ball. This stretching or squeezing is called the Doppler effect, so the guns are sometimes called Doppler radar guns. Guns like these have shown that top male tennis stars like Mark Phillipousis serve at over 140 mph (230 km/h).

Women tennis stars serve at over 90 mph (150 km/h).

As the ball passes the second pencil, stop the watch and make a note of the time. Roll the ball over the same course ten times, timing it with the stopwatch each time. Try to roll as near the same speed as you can each time. See if you can make each run of the ball exactly the same time. Then measure out a different distance and time the ball over this distance.

GETTING FASTER

To take off, this US airforce F-15E Eagle uses its powerful jets to accelerate from standstill to 200 mph (320 km/h) in less than half a minute.

Few things keep moving at precisely the same speed for long. Nearly all moving objects slow down or speed up eventually. Positive acceleration is speeding up. Negative acceleration, or deceleration, is slowing down.

Acceleration is basically the change in speed over a particular time period. If the speed is measured in feet per second, the acceleration is how much that speed changes in each second—that is, feet per second per second. This can be written as feet per second squared, or ft/s^2.

Scientists describe acceleration as a change in

In focus

CALCULATING ACCELERATION

The change in velocity as things get faster or slow down is the difference between the final velocity (v) *and* the initial velocity (u)—that is, v minus u. The acceleration is how quickly this change in velocity happens. So the acceleration (a) is v minus u divided by the time (t), or:

$$a = (v - u)/t$$

If you know the initial velocity and the acceleration, you can work out how fast something is going after a certain time using this formula:

$$v = u + at$$

In the real world

THROWING A BALL

Throwing a ball in the air means using muscle power to give it acceleration. When a ball is thrown in the air, the throw accelerates it upward, but gravity tries to accelerate it downward. The ball will only travel upward if the positive upward acceleration from the throw is more than the negative, downward acceleration of gravity. The ball falls back down as soon as the downward acceleration exceeds the upward.

A flying basketball is always balanced between the positive acceleration of the throw and the negative acceleration of gravity.

velocity rather than speed. Like velocity, acceleration is a vector quantity—that is, it always happens in a particular direction as well as at a particular rate.

Indeed, acceleration can simply be a change in direction, rather than a change in speed. All circular motion—from an orbiting planet to a spinning bicycle wheel—is acceleration. This is because the direction is always changing.

In most everyday events, the rate at which things accelerate is rarely steady. In a few situations, though, acceleration is constant —that is, the change in velocity and direction is unvarying. The best known example of constant acceleration is gravity. Gravity always makes things fall at the same rate and in the same direction: downward.

UNDERSTANDING ACCELERATION

You will need

- Several sheets of plain white paper
- A compass
- Food coloring or ink
- A small toy truck or car
- Scissors
- A stopwatch
- An empty soda bottle
- A plank of wood
- A tape measure

1 Cut the cone-shaped top off the soda bottle with scissors. The bottle top will be your ink reservoir.

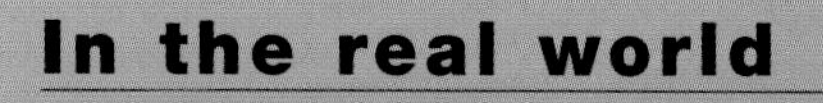

In the real world

GRAVITY ACCELERATION

The earth's gravity accelerates things downward. The truck in this experiment is accelerated down the ramp by the pull of gravity. When things are falling freely, they all experience the same acceleration due to gravity, gaining speed at 32 ft per second per second (9.8 m/s^2). After falling 0.1 seconds, a ball would have fallen barely 2 inches and be falling just 3 ft per second. After falling for 0.3 seconds, it would have fallen 17 inches and reached 10 ft per second. After just 0.6 seconds, it has fallen 5 ft and reached 20 ft per second.

3 Tape the bottle top as upright as possible to the back of the toy truck, with the cap downward.

2 With an adult watching, make a very small hole in the bottle cap with the point of a compass.

Cover the plank with paper. Hold your finger over the hole in the bottle cap, then pour a little food color or ink into the bottle top. With your finger still over the hole, set the truck at the top of the ramp, gently lifting to provide a very slight incline. Let the truck go, and watch the ink drops it leaves behind as it accelerates down the slope.

What is happening?

As something accelerates and travels faster, it covers a greater distance in each time period. Here, the drops of ink fall from the truck at a steady rate. Yet as the truck rolls down the slope, the ink drops get farther and farther apart, showing it is traveling farther and farther in the same time. This means it must be accelerating. This experiment is simple in theory, but it can be hard to make work well. The longer and more gentle the slope, the better it will work. Check that the cap drips ink evenly. Start with the hole too small, then enlarge it.

STARTING TO MOVE

Nothing moves of its own accord. Every object is said to have inertia, and only moves if it is forced to. If anything starts to move, it is because some force is pushing or pulling on it, overcoming its inertia.

Similarly, any moving object goes on moving for the same rate forever, in the same direction. It only varies its pace or direction if something forces it to slow down, speed up, or change course. This tendency to keep going at the same speed is called momentum. Momentum is what throws passengers forward when a car suddenly slams on its brakes.

Inertia and momentum mean there is never any change in an object's motion unless some force accelerates it to a new velocity or in a new direction.

Rollerbladers need much more muscle power to start moving. Once moving, their momentum helps keep them going with much less effort.

Did you know?

Momentum is mass times velocity. The standard science units for momentum are kilogram meters per second or kg.m/s. So a 1,000 kg car moving at 20 m/s would have a momentum of 20,000 kg.m/s. Momentum could also be measured in pound feet per second.

In focus

NEWTON'S LAWS OF MOTION

Isaac Newton (1643-1727) was one of the greatest scientists. In 1665, he worked out three laws of motion. These laws underpin modern science and are used to understand the motion of anything from atoms to galaxies. The First Law is about inertia and momentum, and says an object accelerates or slows down only when a force is applied. The Second Law says that the acceleration depends on mass and force—that is, how heavy the object is and how hard it is being pushed or pulled. The Third Law is about how forces interact. It says that when a force pushes or acts one way, an equal force pushes in the opposite direction.

Newton's discoveries remain the foundation of science today.

The effect of a force on an object depends on the object's mass. Mass is how heavy something is—or more exactly, how much matter it contains.

For scientists, there is no real difference between something moving at a steady speed and something completely still. With both there is no change without a force. So they use the word inertia to describe the tendency of an object to resist a change in velocity, whether it is still or moving. An object's inertia depends on its mass alone. The greater its mass, the greater its inertia and the less effect a certain force has on its motion.

Momentum, however, only applies to moving objects. When something is moving, the force needed to change its motion depends not only on its mass but its velocity, too. The faster and heavier an object is, the greater its momentum, and so the less effect a certain force has on its motion. Momentum is defined as the mass of an object multiplied by its velocity.

When two objects collide, they keep the same combined momentum. Their combined mass times their combined velocity is always the same, even if the balance between them shifts. So whatever momentum one object loses in the collision, the other gains. If one marble hits another, for instance, it may slow down or stop, but as it does, it passes on some or all of its momentum to the other. This is called the conservation of linear momentum.

BEATING INERTIA

You will need

- A large soda bottle (unopened or refilled with water)
- Rubber bands
- Food coloring (optional)

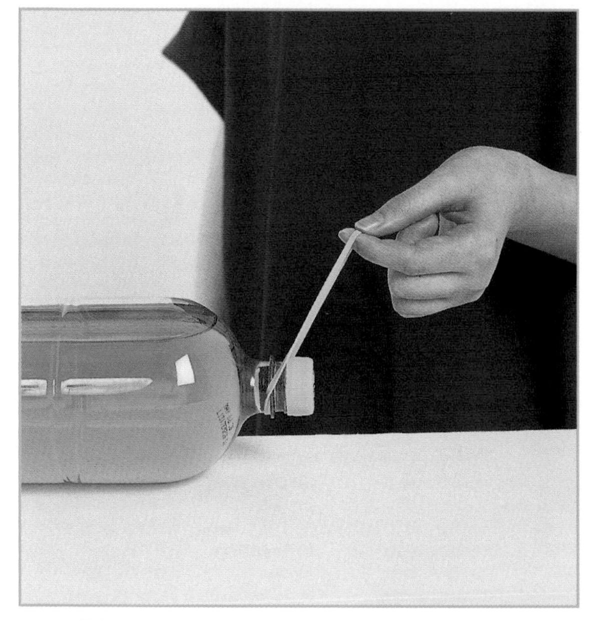

1 Place the bottle on a smooth, flat table. Loop the rubber band around the neck of the bottle. Apply glue if needed.

In the real world

WRECKING BALL

One of the most dramatic uses of momentum is the demolition or wrecking ball used to knock down concrete and brick buildings and other structures. A huge steel ball weighing up to 13,500 lbs (over 6,000 kg) is hung from the jib of a crane. The crane then swivels to swing the ball against the building. The huge weight of the wrecking ball means that it has tremendous momentum, even when swinging quite slowly. A long, fast swing can build up enough momentum to crash against the building with enough force to knock through solid concrete.

A wrecking ball demonstrates clearly the momentum of a heavy object when moving.

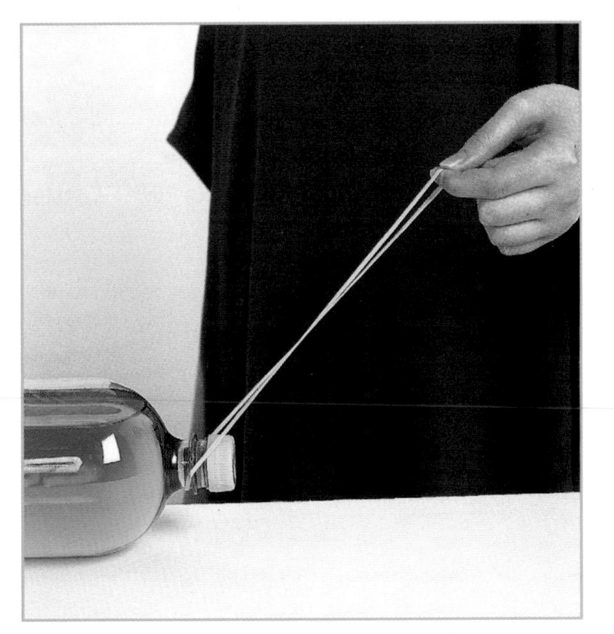

2 Tug the band gently to drag the bottle. Keep pulling until it just starts to move. See how much the band stretches.

What is happening?

The stretching of the rubber band is a simple measure of how much force is needed to drag the bottle. The band is most stretched just before the bottle starts to move. This shows how a great deal of force is needed to overcome an object's inertia and get it moving. Once it is moving steadily, the band gets much shorter. This shows that much less force is needed to keep an object moving. This is because it now has momentum to keep it going. But to accelerate it, you have to apply a lot of force again, stretching the band once more.

Keep pulling gently as the bottle gradually starts to move and continue to pull gently. Try to make the bottle move as smoothly and steadily as possible. Once it is moving evenly, look at how much the band is stretched. It should be much less stretched than when the bottle just started to move in Step 2 above. Now suddenly try to move the bottle faster. What happens to the band?

FORCE AND ACCELERATION

When a baseball player hits the ball, the force of the swinging bat accelerates the ball. The large mass of the bat compared to the lightness of the ball means the ball can often rocket away into the outfield at tremendous speeds.

An object's inertia means it won't start moving without a force acting on it. Nor will it go faster or slower, or change direction, without a force acting on it. The force may change the object's velocity or direction.

A force can be thought of as something that accelerates an object—a push or pull that makes it move faster or slower or veer off in a new direction.

The amount of acceleration that a force creates depends on two things: the size of the force, and the mass of the object. The larger the force, the greater the acceleration. Pushing twice as hard on the pedals of a bicycle, for example, doubles the

Did you know?

The standard units of force are newtons. One newton is the force needed to accelerate 1 kg by 1 m/s^2. Force used to be measured in poundals. A poundal is 0.1383 newtons, or the force needed to accelerate 1 lb by 1 ft/s^2.

bicycle's acceleration. The acceleration is directly proportional to the force.

The effect of the force, however, varies according to the mass. A throw of the same force accelerates a light tennis ball much more than a heavy stone. To accelerate the stone at the same rate as the ball, it has to be thrown with much greater force. So acceleration is also directly proportional to mass.

Forces always act in a particular direction. If you throw a ball forward, the ball is accelerated forward. But objects are very rarely subjected to just a single force. Usually, several forces act on an object, each pulling or pushing the object in a different direction.

The combined effect of these forces is called the resultant. The resultant is midway between all the forces. If one force pulls a bicycle to the left, and an equal force pulls it to the right, the bicycle goes straight on. But if the force pulling it to the left is stronger, the bicycle veers more to the left.

In focus

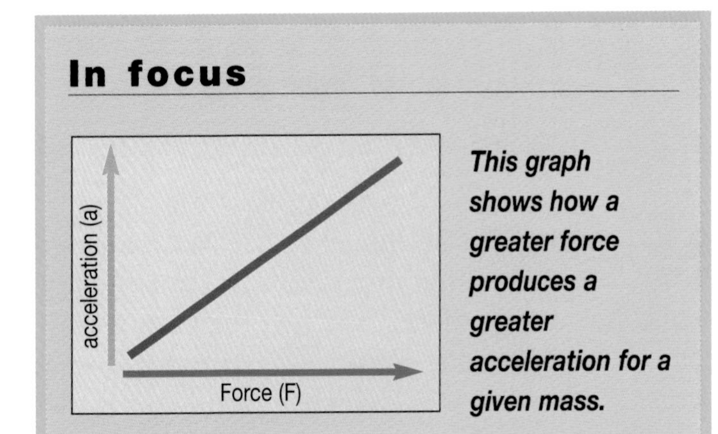

This graph shows how a greater force produces a greater acceleration for a given mass.

FORCE EQUATION

The relationship between force (F), mass (m) and acceleration (a) is summed up in the equation:

$$F = ma$$

This shows the force of an object depends on the combination of its mass and acceleration. This is why the impact of a slow-moving truck and a fast-moving bullet are equally devastating. Both have tremendous force—the truck because of its large mass, the bullet because of its huge acceleration. The equation can also be swapped:

$$a = F/m$$

This shows the acceleration goes up with the force but down with the mass.

FRICTION

Not all forces make things move; some bring them to a halt. A moving object's momentum should mean it carries on moving at the same speed unless some force slows it down. Theoretically, it could go on moving forever.

Yet most things do slow down eventually. Nobody can throw a ball more than a few hundred feet, for instance. Nor has any body yet made a perpetual motion machine—a machine that goes on turning forever under its own momentum.

Racing cyclists try to cut friction with the air by wearing shiny clothes and streamlined helmets.

The reason is that forces slow things down. The main stopping force is friction. Friction is the force between two things rubbing together, and it occurs in almost every situation where things move.

When two solids rub together, jagged places on each surface catch together. These jagged places are clearly visible ridges and snags. But there are often microscopic jagged places even on apparently smooth surfaces. Sometimes the friction can be caused by the attraction between tiny molecules in each surface.

When a ball flies through the air, the friction is created by constant collisions between the ball and air molecules. The ball falls back to the ground as this friction slows it down enough for gravity to pull it down.

Friction tends to make things hot, because much of the energy of a moving object's momentum is converted into heat as the object slows down. Friction can also create noise, as the energy is turned into sounds, such as rubbing and scratching noises.

Sometimes friction is helpful. Without friction, people could not walk on the pavement without their feet sliding as if on ice. Friction makes car tires to grip the road. If tires didn't grip, cars could never brake or even turn corners.

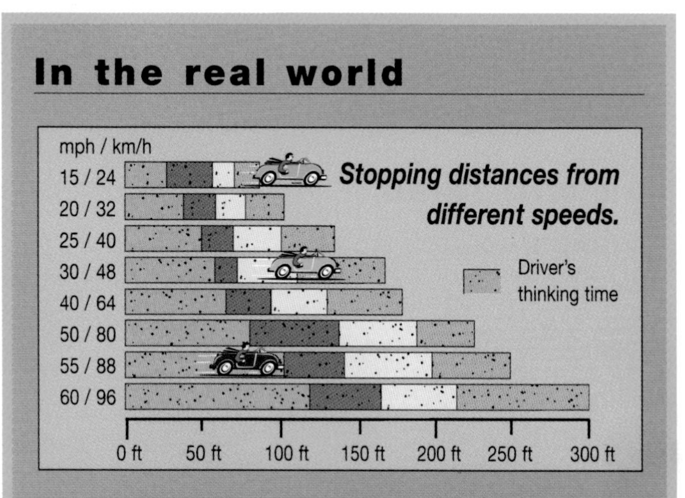

CAR STOPPING DISTANCES

Cars rely on friction to slow down and stop. Their brakes slow the wheels using friction, with pads rubbing against discs on each wheel. The wheels slow the whole car down, relying on friction between the tires and the road. The distance needed to stop a car depends not only on the speed and weight of the car and the efficiency of its brakes, but also the condition of the road. It takes much longer to stop a car on a slippery, wet road than on a dry one.

Often, friction is a problem. It impairs the efficiency of car engines, turning motion into heat. It also makes it hard to slide a heavy object such as a washing machine across a floor.

The amount of friction between two surfaces depends on the two materials and how hard they are pushed together. The amount of friction between two materials is given a rating called the coefficient of friction. Rubber sliding on concrete has a coefficient of 0.8, which is high. Teflon sliding on steel is 0.04, which is very low.

ROUGH AND SMOOTH

You will need

- A plank of wood
- A ruler
- A small wooden toy block
- Scotch tape

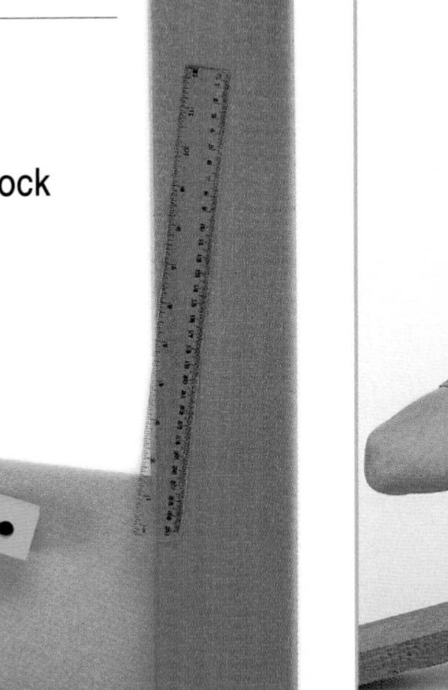

1 Place the toy block on the plank. Lift the plank up gradually until the block starts to slide down the slope.

In focus

The pressure of a skate blade melts ice, creating a film of water for the skate to run on, so skaters slide easily over the ice.

REDUCING FRICTION

Friction between two surfaces can be reduced by lubrication. Lubrication means putting a substance such as oil or water between the two surfaces. This keeps the two surfaces very slightly apart, allowing them to slide over each other more easily. Ice is slippery because the top surface melts, creating a film of water that reduces friction.

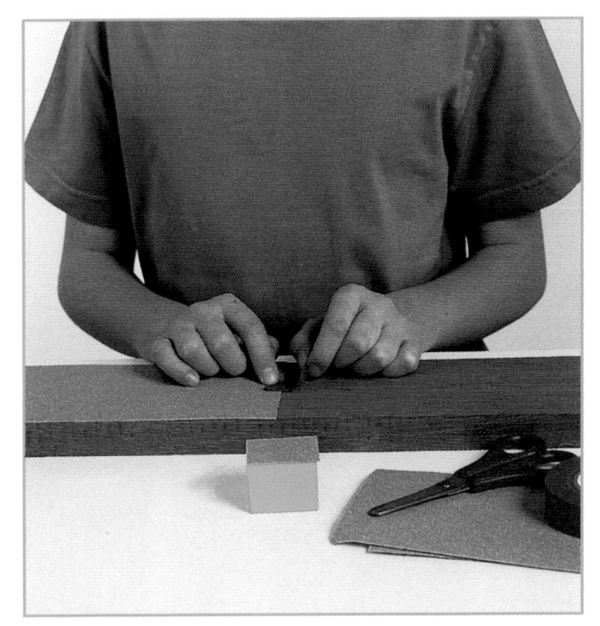

3 Stick sandpaper on the top side of the plank. Stick a small square of sandpaper to the toy block.

2 Measure the height of the plank at the point where the block starts to slide.

What is happening?

The greater the friction between two surfaces, the greater force is needed to overcome it and make the objects move. Because the block and plank are smooth, the friction between them is low. So, as the measurement in Step 2 shows, the toy block slides when the slope is gentle and the force of gravity pulling the block down the slope is weak. Putting sandpaper on each surface increases the friction. The grains of sand on each surface interlock and stop them sliding together. So the slope must be much steeper and the force of gravity greater to overcome the friction and make the block slide.

Place the toy block on the plank at the same point as in Step 2, with the sandpaper side facing down. Lift the plank up gradually until the block begins to slide down the slope. You may find the brick never slides, but simply tips over. Measure the height of the slope when the block just begins to slide or tip over.

ACTION AND REACTION

Every time two objects come in contact, they interact. As they touch, they exert forces on each other. When someone walks, their feet push down on the ground and the ground pushes back up with exactly the same force. If the ground reacted with any less force, the feet would sink into the ground. If the ground pushed harder, it would push the feet up.

When the oars of a boat push on the water, the water pushes back with equal force. If it did not react like this, only the water would move, and the boat would stay still.

Did you know?

When fired, guns recoil. As the gases from the gunpowder expand, the gun pushes the bullet forward and the bullet pushes the gun back equally. Because the bullet is so much lighter, the bullet is accelerated much more, but the gun can still give a powerful kick back.

In fact, whenever anything moves or interacts, there is always this balance of opposing forces—an "action" force that pushes, and a "reaction" force that pushes back with exactly the same force in the opposite direction. Newton's Third Law of Motion puts it this way: "For every action, there is an equal and opposite reaction."

This action-reaction force pair can be seen in all kinds of situations. When an oarsman pulls on his oars, for instance, the oars push the water back as they dip into the water. If the water did not react, it would simply be pushed backward and the boat would not move. But the water reacts by pushing back on the oars with equal force, driving the boat forward. So while the water moves back, the boat moves forward.

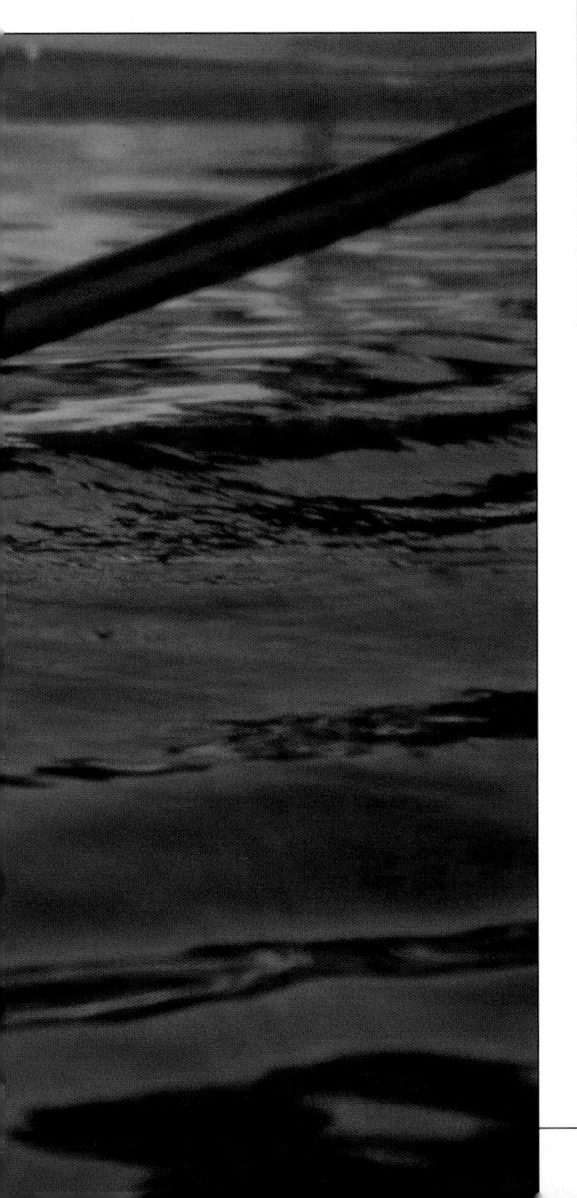

In focus

DOES THE EARTH MOVE?

When two things interact, the law of action and reaction means both push each other with equal force in opposite directions. But this does not mean they both move equally; how much each moves depends on its relative mass. A runner drives the world backward with his feet with the same force that he drives himself forward. But the world is so massive, the effect of this force is very tiny, so the runner accelerates much more than the world.

The world does move when someone steps on it, but only very, very slightly.

Similarly, as the wheels of a bicycle turn, they try to push the road back. The road reacts by pushing the wheels forward, and so the bicycle moves along the road.

REACTION ROCKETS

You will need

- ✓ A cork
- ✓ A craft knife
- ✓ Glue
- ✓ An empty soda bottle
- ✓ Three "fins" cut from balsa wood to match the curved top of the bottle
- ✓ A sports ball inflator

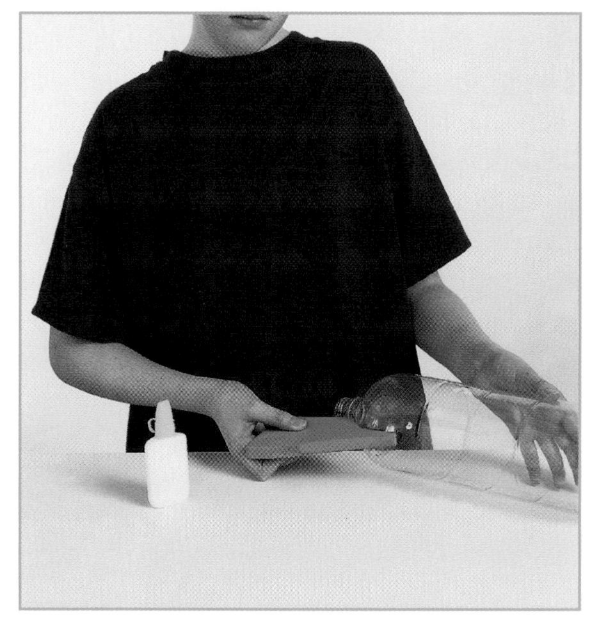

1 Glue the fins firmly to the top of the bottle. Take care that each fin is straight, in line with the bottle.

In focus

HOW ROCKETS MOVE THROUGH SPACE

On Earth, cars, trucks, and trains all move forward because they have something to push against, using the principle of action and reaction. Even planes and rockets push against the air. So how do space rockets move through empty space where there is nothing to push against? In fact, they still use the same principle of action and reaction. But the reaction here is between the body of the rocket and the burning gases swelling out behind it. The reaction between them thrusts the rocket forward and the gases backward.

When the space shuttle roars up into the air, it is propelled by the blast of gases pushing on the air.

What is happening?

This water rocket fires the bottle powerfully into the air using action and reaction. As you pump air into the bottle, the air pressure inside builds up until it pops the cork. As the cork pops, the pressurized air suddenly expands. The air pushes on the water and the water on the air in an action and reaction. Because the bottle and air are very much lighter than the water, they are accelerated up much more than the water is pushed down.

2 Make a hole through the cork with the nozzle of the inflator. Clear any cork lodged in the inflator with a pin.

Fill the bottle one-quarter full with water. Push the cork into the bottle with the inflator nozzle inward. Take the bottle outside into an open space, well away from houses and overhead wires. Stand the bottle upside down. Keeping your distance, pump air into the bottle. The pressure builds up until the cork pops and the rocket shoots upwards.

HIGH SPEED MOTION

Subatomic particles move far too quick to see, but as they speed through clouds of superheated vapor in a bubble chamber, they leave the little trails of bubbles visible in this picture.

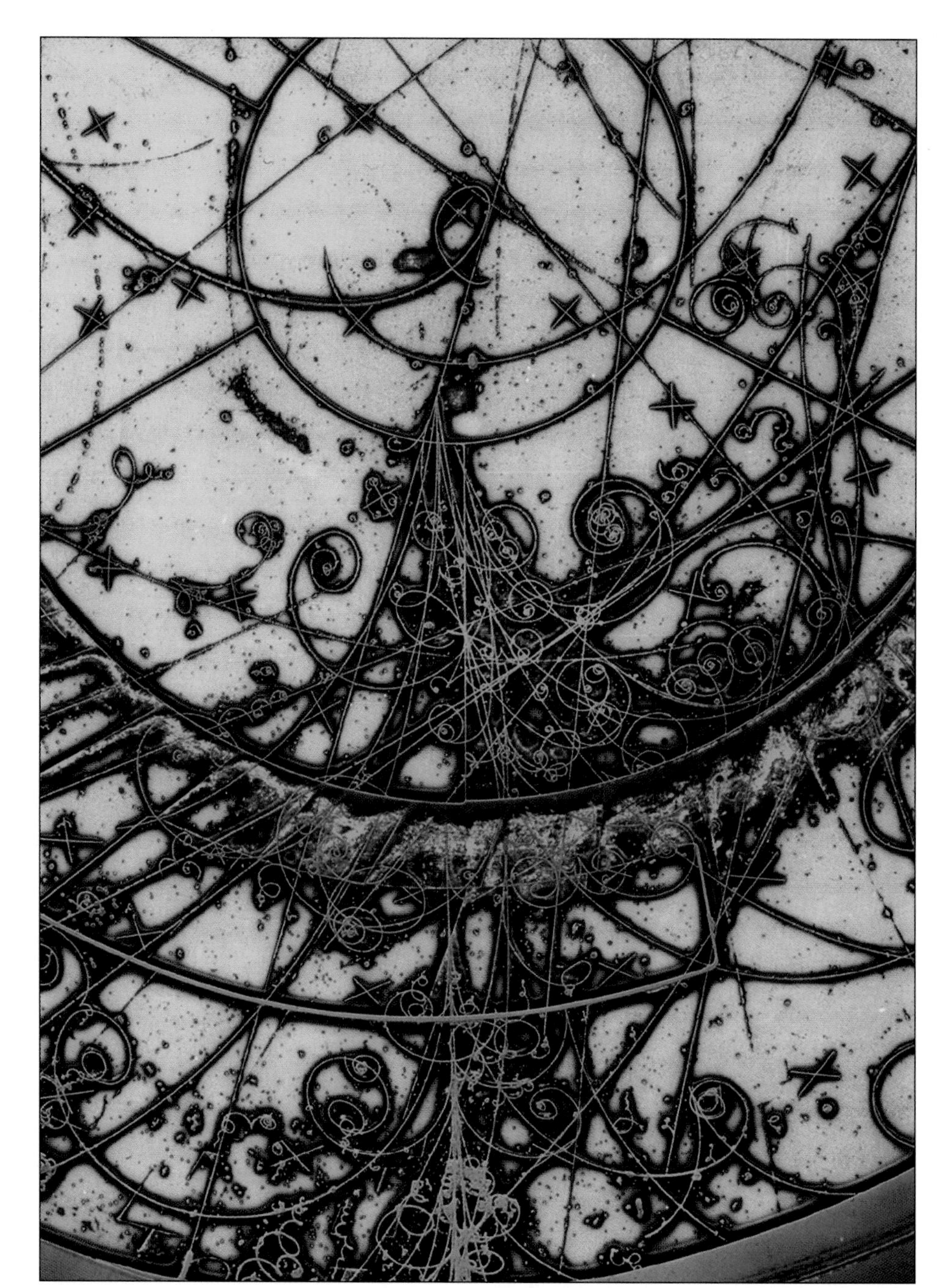

Less than two centuries ago, the fastest things anybody really knew about were birds. Nobody had ever travelled faster than on a galloping horse. Now high-speed trains can whisk people along the ground at speeds of over 300 mph (500 km/h) and the Concorde jet can carry passengers through the air over twice as fast as sound, cruising at 1,450 mph (2,333 km/h).

Spaceships have taken astronauts to dramatically higher speeds. The crew of the *Apollo 10* spacecraft reached 24,791 mph (39,897 km/h) on their way to the Moon. Future spaceflights to Mars may see even higher speeds achieved.

Using special equipment, scientists have discovered a huge array of motion at such high speeds that it cannot normally be seen. 150 years ago, Eadward Muybridge tried stop-motion photography for the first time. Using brief flashes of light, he could freeze the motion of galloping horses. Now photos can capture even faster events. The world's fastest cameras use laser lights to see the molecules moving in chemical reactions lasting just one femtosecond, or 0.000000000000001 seconds.

In space, scientists have found many objects moving at previously unimaginable speeds. The earth itself moves around the Sun at 66,620 mph (107,210 km/h), but this is quite slow in space terms. A spiral nebula (gas cloud) known as NGC 7619 is hurtling away from Earth at over 2,348 miles (3,779 km) per second! This is the fastest known motion in the universe for anything above the subatomic level.

In focus

MOVING PARTICLES

The fastest thing in the universe is light, which travels 186,000 miles (300,000 km) a second. But other subatomic particles (particles smaller than atoms) can travel very fast too. On average, electrons whizzing around the nucleus of every atom travel at about 1,400 miles (2,200 km) a second. In special machines called particle accelerators, scientists can accelerate particles almost to the speed of light, but not quite. The speed of light is the ultimate speed. Einstein's theory of relativity shows that as objects approach the speed of light, they get heavier and heavier. To reach these very high speeds, scientists need to use more and more energy. These speeds are usually measured in terms of the energy needed, in eV or electron volts. Accelerating an electron to 90 percent of light's speed needs 220,000 eV. Accelerating it to 99.9999992 percent calls for 4 billion eV or 4 GeV.

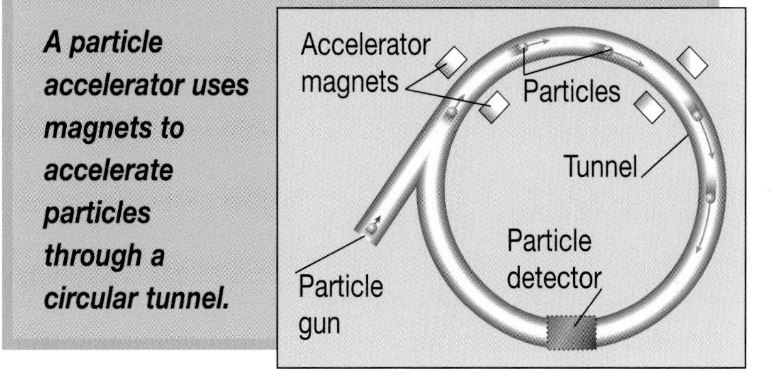

A particle accelerator uses magnets to accelerate particles through a circular tunnel.

Experiments in Science

Science is about knowledge: it is concerned with knowing and trying to understand the world around us. The word comes from the Latin word, *scire,* to know.

In the early 17th century, the great English thinker Francis Bacon suggested that the best way to learn about the world was not simply to think about it, but to go out and look for yourself—to make observations and try things out. Ever since then, scientists have tried to approach their work with a mixture of observation and experiment. Scientists insist that an idea or theory must be tested by observation and experiment before it is widely accepted.

All the experiments in this book have been tried before, and the theories behind them are widely accepted. But that is no reason why you should accept them. Once you have done all the experiments in this book, you will know the ideas are true not because we have told you so, but because you have seen for yourself.

All too often in science there is an external factor interfering with the result which the scientist just has not thought of. Sometimes this can make the experiment seem to work when it has not, as well as making it fail. One scientist conducted lots of demonstrations to show that a clever horse called Hans could count things and tap out the answer with his hoof. The horse was indeed clever, but later it was found that rather than counting, he was getting clues from tiny unconscious movements of the scientist's eyebrows.

This is why it is very important when conducting experiments to be as rigorous as you possibly can. The more casual you are, the more "eyebrow factors" you will let in. There will always be some things that you can not control. But the more precise you are, the less these are likely to affect the outcome.

What went wrong?

However careful you are, your experiments may not work. If so, you should try to find out where you went wrong. Then repeat the experiment until you are absolutely sure you are doing everything right. Scientists learn as much, if not more, from experiments that go wrong as those that succeed. In 1929, Alexander Fleming discovered the first antibiotic drug, penicillin, when he noticed that a bacteria culture he was growing for an experiment had gone moldy—and that the mold seemed to kill the bacteria. A poor scientist would probably have thrown the moldy culture away. A good scientist is one who looks for alternative explanations for unexpected results.

Glossary

acceleration: In everyday language, acceleration is a gain in speed. Scientifically, it is a change in velocity over a certain time. It can mean either a loss or gain in speed or a change in direction, or both.

coefficient of friction: A measure of the force that is needed to overcome the friction between two rubbing surfaces.

deceleration: Slowing down or scientifically, a reduction in velocity in the direction an object is traveling.

Doppler effect: The way sound or light waves are squeezed as an object moves towards you and are stretched as the object moves away. This is heard in the changing pitch in the siren of a passing police car.

dynamics: The study of the way objects move when forced to.

force: Any push or pull that accelerates an object to a new velocity or changes the object's shape.

friction: The force which stops two touching surfaces sliding past each other.

gravity: The force of attraction between every bit of matter in the universe. The greater the mass, the greater the attraction. Gravity is what makes things fall to the ground.

inertia: The natural tendency of an object to stay still or keep moving in the same direction or speed, unless forced to accelerate. Inertia is equivalent to mass. The heavier an object, the greater its inertia, and the more force is needed to accelerate it.

linear: In a straight line.

lubrication: Insertion of fluid such as oil between two surfaces to reduce friction.

momentum: The natural tendency of a moving object to stay moving. It is the mass of an object multiplied by its velocity. The faster an object is moving and the heavier its mass, the greater its momentum will be.

newton: Standard scientific unit of force: the force needed to accelerate a mass of 1 kilogram by 1 meter per second per second.

particle: Invisibly tiny bits such as atoms from which all things are made.

resultant: The acceleration of an object resulting from the combination of two or more forces.

rotational: Moving in a circle.

scalar quantity: A measurement which has a size but no direction, such as speed and mass.

speed: The rate something is moving, measured by the distance traveled divided by the time. It is scalar because it has no direction.

vector: A measurement which has both size and direction, such as velocity and acceleration.

velocity: The rate something is moving in a particular direction. It is a vector because it has direction.

Index

THE CHICAGO PUBLIC LIBRARY